The Wicked Book

of

REALLY GOOD
JOKES

The Wicked Book
of
REALLY GOOD
JOKES

p

This is a Parragon Book
This edition published in 2001

Parragon
Queen Street House
4 Queen Street
Bath BA1 1HE, UK

Produced by Magpie Books, an imprint of
Constable & Robinson Ltd, London

ISBN 0-75255-442-5

A copy of the British Library Cataloguing-in-Publication Data
is available from the British Library

Printed and bound in the EC

Contents

Introduction

This Wicked book contains hundreds of really good howlers to keep you roaring with laughter. Why not amuse yourself and your friends by asking such questions as How can a teacher double his money? (by folding it in half). Did you know how to tell that owls are cleverer than chickens? Well, have you ever heard of Kentucky Fried Owl? There are hundreds of jokes here to get you and your friends chuckling away as you read through.

Farm
Animals

What do you get if you cross a worm with a young goat?
A dirty kid.

Waiter, this food isn't fit for a pig!
All right, I'll get you some that is.

What do you get if you cross a snake with a pig?
A boar constrictor.

What do you get if you cross a monster
with a cow and an oat field?
Lumpy porridge.

What happened to the vampire who
swallowed a sheep?
He felt baaaaaaaaaaaaaad.

Visitor: Wow, you have a lot of flies
buzzing round your horses and cows. Do
you ever shoo them?
Rancher: No, we just let them go barefoot.

Joe: Did you ever see a horse fly?
Pete: No, but I once saw a cow jump off a cliff.

"I told you to draw a picture of a cow eating grass," said the art master. "Why have you handed in a blank sheet of paper?"
"Because the cow ate all the grass, that's why there's no grass." "But what about the cow?"
"There wasn't much point in it hanging around when there was nothing to eat, so he went back to the barn."

"What did the doctor say to you yesterday?" asked the teacher.

"He said I was allergic to horses." "I've never heard of anyone suffering from that. What's the condition called?"

"Bronco-itis."

"I asked you to draw a pony and trap," said the art master. "You've only drawn the pony. Why?"

"Well, sir. I thought the pony would draw the trap."

What's a sheep's hairdresser called?
A baa-baa shop.

Why should a school not be near a chicken farm?
To avoid the pupils overhearing fowl language.

The teacher was furious with her son. "Just because you've been put in my class, there's no need to think you can take liberties. You're a pig." The boy said nothing. "Well! Do you know what a pig is?" "Yes, Mom," said the boy. "The offspring of a swine."

Did you hear about the idiot who made his chickens drink boiling water?
He thought they would lay hard-boiled eggs.

An idiot decided to start a chicken farm so he bought a hundred chickens. A month later he returned to the dealer for another hundred chickens because all of the first lot had died. A month later he was back at the dealer's for another hundred chickens for the second lot had also died. "But I think I know where I'm going wrong," said the idiot, "I think I'm planting them too deep."

What happened when the ghostly cows got out of their field?
There was udder chaos.

What does a headless horseman ride?
A nightmare.

Mary had a bionic cow,
It lived on safety pins.
And every time she milked that
  cow,
The milk came out in tins.

On which side does a chicken have the most feathers?
On the outside.

Two friends who lived in the town were chatting. "I've just bought a pig," said the first.
"But where will you keep it?" said the second. "Your garden's much too small for a pig!"
"I'm going to keep it under my bed," replied his friend.
"But what about the smell?
"He'll soon get used to that."

Dad, that Mr Jenkins down the road said you weren't fit to live with pigs!
What did you say, son?
I stuck up for you. I said you were certainly fit to live with pigs.

The Stock Market is a place where sheep and cattle are sold.

What did the neurotic pig say to the farmer?
You take me for grunted.

Doctor, doctor, I've got a little stye.
Then you'd better buy a little pig.

Dim Dinah wrote in her exercise book:
Margarine is butter made from imitation
cows.

How do phantom hens dance?
Chick to chick.

School's Out

Barry: Who was that I saw you with last night?
Larry: It was a girl from the school.
Barry: Teacher?
Larry: Didn't have to!

Mary's class was taken to the Natural History Museum in London. "Did you enjoy yourself?" asked her mother when she got home.
"Oh yes," replied Mary. "But it was funny going to a dead zoo."

"Dad," said Billy to his father who was a bank robber, "I need $50 for the school trip tomorrow."
"OK, son," said his dad, "I'll get you the cash when the bank closes."

Alex's class went on a nature study ramble.
"What do you call a thing with ten legs, red spots and great big jaws, Sir?" asked Alex.
"I've no idea, why do you ask?" replied the teacher.
"Because one just crawled up your trouser leg."

Mother: Did you enjoy the school outing, dear?
Jane: Yes. And we're going again tomorrow.
Mother: Really? Why's that?
Jane: To try and find the kids we left behind.

A teacher took her class for a walk in the country, and Susie found a snake. "Come quickly, Miss," she called, "here's a tail without a body!"

How do insects travel when they go on vacation?
They go for a buggy ride.

The class went to a concert. After, Jacqui asked the music teacher why members of the orchestra kept looking at a book while they played. "Those books are the score," replied the teacher. "Really?" replied Jacqui, "who was winning?"

At Christmas the school went to a special service in church. The teacher asked if they had enjoyed it, and if they had behaved themselves. "Oh yes, Miss," said Brenda. "A lady came round and offered us a plateful of money, but we all said no thank you."

The class was taken to vist the opera, and afterwards young Daniel was asked if he had enjoyed it.

"Oh, yes," he replied. "But why did that man with a stick keep hitting that lady?"

"He wasn't hitting her, he was conducting the orchestra," said his teacher.

"But if he wasn't hitting her, why was she screaming?" asked Daniel.

What do you call a mosquito on vacation?
An itch-hiker.

"Why did you come back early from your
vacation?" one of Alec's classmates asked
him.

"Well, on the first day we were there one
of the chickens died and that night we had
chicken soup. The next day one of the pigs
died and we had pork chops . . ."

"But why did you come back?"

"Well, on the third day the farmer's
father-in-law died. What would you have
done?"

Did you hear what Dumb Donald did when he offered to paint the garage for his dad in the summer vacation? The instructions said put on three coats, so he went in and put on his blazer, his raincoat and his duffle coat.

Harry was telling his classmate about his vacation in Switzerland. His friend had never been to Switzerland, and asked, "What did you think of the scenery?" "Oh, I couldn't see much," Harry admitted. "There were all those mountains in the way."

Where do ghosts go on vacation?
The Dead Sea.

How do toads travel?
By hoppercraft.

Teacher: Now, remember, children, travel
is very good for you. It broadens the mind.
Sarah, muttering: If you're anything to go
by, that's not all it broadens!

What do demons have on vacation?
A devil of a time.

My teacher is so stupid she thinks that aroma is someone who travels a lot.

The pupils in the twelfth grade, who had learned to type, were being interviewed by prospective employers. Lisa was asked her typing speed. "I'm not sure," she replied. "But I can rub out at fifty words a minute."

Suresh: Whatever will Clive do when he leaves school? I can't see him being bright enough to get a job.
Sandra: He could always be a ventriloquist's dummy.

Where do ants go on vacation?
Fr-ants

"You never get anything right," complained the teacher. "What kind of job do you think you'll get when you leave school?"
"Well, I want to be the weather girl on TV."

Sarah: Did you hear about Samantha now she's left school? She's working for a company that makes blotting paper.
Selina: Does she enjoy it?
Sarah: I believe she finds it very absorbing.

When I was in school I was as smart as the next fellow.
What a pity the next fellow was such an idiot.

When you leave school, you should become a bone specialist.
You've certainly got the head for it.

Sid: Mom, all the boys in school call me Big Head.

Mom: Never mind, love, just pop down to the fruit and vegetable store and collect the 10 pounds of potatoes I ordered in your cap.

Mother: How was your first day in school?

Little Boy: OK, but I haven't got my present yet.

Mother: What do you mean?

Little Boy: Well the teacher gave me a chair, and said "Sit there for the present."

A little boy came home from his first day at kindergarten and said to his mother. "What's the use of going to school? I can't read, I can't write and the teacher won't let me talk."

Two little girls at a very posh school were talking to each other. "I told the chauffeur to take his peaked cap off in case the other girls here thought I was a snob," said the first.

"How strange," said the second. "I told mine to keep his on in case anyone thought he was my father."

Really Good Knock, Knock Jokes

Knock knock.
Who's there?
Ada.
Ada who?
Ada lot for breakfast.

Knock knock.
Who's there?
Aleta.
Aleta who?
Aleta from your bank manager.

Knock knock.
Who's there?
Alma.
Alma who?
Alma lovin'.

Knock knock.
Who's there?
Althea.
Althea who?
Althea in court.

Knock knock.
Who's there?
Amanda.
Amanda who?
Amanda the table.

Knock knock.
Who's there?
Amber.
Amber who?
Amberter than I was yesterday.

Knock knock.
Who's there?
Amy.
Amy who?
Amy for the top.

Knock knock.
Who's there?
Anna.
Anna who?
Annamazingly good joke.

Knock knock.
Who's there?
Annabel.
Annabel who?
Annabel would be useful on this door.

Knock knock.
Who's there?
Annette.
Annette who?
Annette curtain looks good in the window.

Knock knock.
Who's there?
Annie.
Annie who?
Annie one you like.

Knock knock.
Who's there?
Anya.
Anya who?
Anya best behavior.

Knock knock.
Who's there?
Audrey.
Audrey who?
Audrey to pay for this?

Knock knock.
Who's there?
Augusta.
Augusta who?
Augustalmost felt like winter.

Knock knock.
Who's there?
Aurora.
Aurora who?
Aurora's just come from a big lion!

Knock knock.
Who's there?
Polly.
Polly who?
Polly the other one, it's got bells on.

Knock knock.
Who's there?
Poppy.
Poppy who?
Poppy'n any time you like.

Knock knock.
Who's there?
Portia.
Portia who?
Portia the door – it's stuck.

Knock knock.
Who's there?
Rena.
Rena who?
Renamok in the shopping mall.

Knock knock.
Who's there?
Renata.
Renata who?
Renata sugar. Can I borrow some?

Knock knock.
Who's there?
Rhona.
Rhona who?
Rhonaround town.

Knock knock.
Who's there?
Rhonda.
Rhonda who?
Rhonda why?

Knock knock.
Who's there?
Rita.
Rita who?
Rita novel.

Knock knock.
Who's there?
Rose.
Rose who?
Rose early one morning.

Knock knock.
Who's there?
Rosina.
Rosina who?
Rosina vase.

Knock knock.
Who's there?
Ruth.
Ruth who?
Ruthless people.

Knock knock.
Who's there?
Saffron.
Saffron who?
Saffron a chair and it collapsed.

Knock knock.
Who's there?
Sally.
Sally who?
Sallyeverything you've got.

Knock knock.
Who's there?
Samantha.
Samantha who?
Samantha baby have gone for a walk.

Knock knock.
Who's there?
Sandra.
Sandra who?
Sandrabout your toes on the beach.

Knock knock.
Who's there?
Sandy.
Sandy who?
Sandy shore.

Knock knock.
Who's there?
Sarah.
Sarah who?
Sarah doctor in the house?

Knock knock.
Who's there?
Serena.
Serena who?
Serena round the corner.

Knock knock.
Who's there?
Sharon.
Sharon who?
Sharon share alike – would you like some of
my chocolate?

Knock knock.
Who's there?
Jessica.
Jessica who?
Jessica lot up last night?

Knock knock.
Who's there?
Joan.
Joan who?
Joan call us, we'll call you.

Knock knock.
Who's there?
Joanna.
Joanna who?
Joanna big kiss?

Knock knock.
Who's there?
Juanita.
Juanita who?
Juanita big meal?

Knock knock.
Who's there?
Judy.
Judy who?
Judy liver newspapers still?

Knock knock.
Who's there?
Julie.
Julie who?
Julie'n on this door a lot?

Knock knock.
Who's there?
Juliet.
Juliet who?
Juliet him get away with that?

Knock knock.
Who's there?
June.
June who?
June know how to open a door?

Knock knock.
Who's there?
Juno.
Juno who?
Juno how to get out of here?

Knock knock.
Who's there?
Justine.
Justine who?
Justine case.

Knock knock.
Who's there.
Nadia.
Nadia who?
Nadia head if you want to come in.

Knock knock.
Who's there?
Nancy.
Nancy who?
Nancy a piece of cake?

Knock knock.
Who's there?
Nicky.
Nicky who?
Nicky nacks.

Knock knock.
Who's there?
Nola.
Nola who?
Nolaner driver may drive a car alone.

Knock knock.
Who's there?
Norma.
Norma who?
Normally the butler opens the door.

Knock knock.
Who's there?
Olga.
Olga who?
Olga home now.

Knock knock.
Who's there?
Olive.
Olive who?
Olive in this house – what are you doing there?

Knock knock.
Who's there?
Olivia.
Olivia who?
Olivia'l is great for cooking.

Knock knock.
Who's there?
Onya.
Onya who?
Onya marks, get set, go.

Knock knock.
Who's there?
Pam.
Pam who?
Pamper yourself.

Knock knock.
Who's there?
Pammy.
Pammy who?
Pammy something nice when you are at the shops!

Knock knock.
Who's there?
Patty.
Patty who?
Patty-cake.

Knock knock.
Who's there?
Peg.
Peg who?
Peg your pardon, I've got the wrong door.

Knock knock.
Who's there?
Penny.
Penny who?
Penny for your thoughts.

Knock knock.
Who's there?
Petal.
Petal who?
Petal fast, we're nearly there.

Knock knock.
Who's there?
Phoebe.
Phoebe who?
Phoebe way above my price.

Knock knock.
Who's there?
Phyllis.
Phyllis who?
Phyllis up.

Knock knock.
Who's there?
Polly.
Polly who?
Polly other one, it's got bells on.

Questions
and Answers

Confucius he say: If teacher ask you question and you not know answer, mumble.

Why is a classroom like an old car? Because it's full of nuts, and has a crank at the front.

Teacher: If you saw me standing by a witch, what fruit would it remind you of?
Pupil: A pear.

What is the most popular sentence at school?
I don't know.

"Why are you tearing up your homework notebook and scattering the pieces around the classroom?" a furious teacher asked one of her pupils.
"To keep the elephants away, Miss."
"There are no elephants."
"Shows how effective it is then, doesn't it?"

What do you get if you cross a caretaker
with an elephant?
A twenty-ton school cleaner.

Why is school like a shower?
One wrong turn and you're in hot water.

Teacher: What did Robert the Bruce do after watching the spider climbing up and down?
Pupil: He invented the yo-yo.

Teacher: Have you ever seen a duchess?
Pupil: Yes – it's the same as an English "s!"

Knock, knock.
Who's there?
Quiet Tina.
Quiet Tina who?
Quiet Tina classroom.

Did you hear about the posh school where all the pupils smelled?
It was for filthy rich kids only.

What are pupils at ghost schools called?
Ghoulboys and ghoulgirls.

What did the ghost teacher say to her class?
Watch the board and I'll go through it again.

"Mary," said her teacher, "you can't bring that lamb into school. What about the smell?"

"Oh, that's all right, Miss," said Mary. "It'll soon get used to it."

A school inspector was talking to a pupil. "How many teachers work in this school?" he asked.

"Only about half of them, I reckon," replied the pupil.

Why should a school not be near a chicken farm?
To avoid the pupils overhearing fowl language.

Kelly: Is God a doctor, Miss?
Teacher: In some ways, Kelly. Why do you ask?
Kelly: Because the Bible says that the Lord gave the tablets to Moses.

"What were you before you came to school, boys and girls?" asked the teacher, hoping that someone would say "Babies." She was disappointed when all the children cried out "Happy!"

Knock, knock.
Who's there?
Teacher.
Teacher who?
Teacher-self French.

Teacher: I was going to read you a story called *The Invasion of the Body Snatchers*, but I've changed my mind.
Class: Oh why, Miss?
Teacher: Because we might get carried away.

The teacher was furious with her son. "Just because you've been put in my class, there's no need to think you can take liberties. You're a pig."

The boy said nothing. "Well! Do you know what a pig is?"

"Yes, Mom," said the boy. "The offspring of a swine."

Teacher: Who can tell me what "dogma" means?

Cheeky Charlie: It's a lady dog that's had puppies, Sir.

"Welcome to school, Simon," said the nursery school teacher to the new boy. "How old are you?"

"I'm not old," said Simon. "I'm nearly new."

"Please, Miss! How do you spell ichael?" The teacher was rather bewildered. "Don't you mean Michael?"

"No, Miss. I've written the 'M' already."

Why are teachers jealous of driving instructors?

Because driving instructors are allowed to belt their pupils.

"Please, Sir! Please, Sir! Why do you keep me locked up in this cage?"
"Because you're the teacher's pet."

The school teacher was furious when Alec knocked him down with his new bicycle in the playground. "Don't you know how to ride that yet?" he roared.
"Oh yes!" shouted Alec over his shoulder. "It's the bell I can't work yet."

Teacher: And did you see the Catskill Mountains on your trip to America?
Jimmy: No, but I saw them kill mice.

Chuck: Do you have holes in your underpants?

Teacher: No, of course not.

Chuck: Then how do you get your feet through?

Teacher: Who can tell me what geese eat?

Paul: Er, gooseberries, Sir?

Teacher: What is the longest night of the year?

Alex: A fortnight.

Tracy: Would you punish someone for something they haven't done?
Teacher: Of course not.
Tracy: Oh good, because I haven't done my homework.

Teacher: What's the difference between a buffalo and a bison?
Student: You can't wash your hands in a buffalo, Miss.

Retired colonel, talking of the good old days: Have you ever hunted bear?
His grandson's teacher: No, but I've been fishing in shorts.

Teacher: What do you know about Lake Erie?
Rose: It's full of ghosts, Miss.

Teacher: And why would you like to be a teacher, Clarence?

Clarence: Because I wouldn't have to learn anything, Sir. I'd know everything by then.

Teacher: Name six things that contain milk.

Dumb Dora: Custard, cocoa, and four cows.

Teacher: Peter! Why are you scratching yourself?

Peter: 'Cos no one else knows where I itch.

Teacher: Who can tell me what an archeologist is?

Tracey: It's someone whose career is in ruins.

Teacher: Why are you late, Penelope?

Penelope: I was obeying the sign that says "Children – Dead Slow," Miss.

Teacher: Who knows what a hippy is?

Clever Dick: It's something that holds your leggy on.

Did you hear about the boy who was told to do 100 lines?
He drew 100 cats on the paper. He thought the teacher had said lions.

Teacher: What's a robin?
John: A bird that steals, Miss.

Teacher: Can anyone tell me what a shamrock is?
Jimmy: It's a fake diamond, Miss.

Knock, knock.
Who's there?
Alison.
Alison who?
Alison to my teacher!

Teacher: Why are you always late?
Roger: I threw away my alarm clock.
Teacher: But why did you throw away your alarm clock?
Roger: Because it always went off when I was asleep.

Teacher: Who can tell me where Turkey is?

Dumb Donald: We ate ours last Christmas, Miss.

Teacher: What is meant by "doggerel?"

Terry: Little dogs, Miss.

Teacher: Why did the Romans build straight roads?
Alex: So the Britons couldn't lie in ambush round the corners.

Boy: Why did you throw my homework in the bin?
Teacher: Because it was trash.

Teacher: Who was the first woman on earth?
Angela: I don't know, Sir.
Teacher: Come on, Angela, it has something to do with an apple.
Angela: Granny Smith?

Teacher: Why do birds fly south in winter?
Jim: Because it's too far to walk.

Teacher: What happened to your homework?
Boy: I made it into a paper plane and someone hijacked it.

Teacher: Why are you standing on your head?
Boy: I'm just trying to turn things over in my mind, Sir.

Teacher: Who can tell me what BC stands for?
Girl: Before calculators.

Girl: Why do you call me pilgrim?
Teacher: Because you're making so little progress.

Teacher: Why did you put that frog in Melinda's case?
Boy: Because I couldn't find a mouse.

Teacher: Billy. Didn't you hear me call you?
Billy: Yes, Miss, but you told us yesterday not to answer back.

Teacher: You seem to be exceedingly ignorant, Williams. Have you read Dickens?
Williams: No, Sir.
Teacher: Have you read Shakespeare?
Williams: No, Sir.
Teacher: Well, what have you read?
Williams: Er . . . er . . . I've red hair, Sir.

Teacher: What is the plural of mouse?
Pupil: Mice.
Teacher: And what is the plural of baby?
Pupil: Twins.

Teacher: Alan, give me a sentence starting with "I."

Alan: I is . . .

Teacher: No, Alan. You must always say "I am."

Alan: Oh right. I am the ninth letter of the alphabet.

Teacher: Spell the word "needle," Kenneth.

Kenneth: N, e, i . . .

Teacher: No, Kenneth, there's no "i" in needle.

Kenneth: Then it's a rotten needle, Miss!

Teacher: Carol, what is "can't" short for?

Carol: Cannot.

Teacher: And what is "don't" short for?

Carol: Doughnut!

Fish and Sea Creatures

Why did the slippery eel blush?
Because the sea weed.

What goes straight up in the air and
wobbles?
A jellyfishcopter.

How do you start a jellyfish race?
Get set!

What do you get if you cross an octopus
with a skunk?
An octopong.

How did the octopus lovers walk down the road?
Arm in arm in arm in arm in arm in arm in arm in arm.

What do you get if you cross a jellyfish with a sheepdog?
Colliewobbles.

What did the octopus say to his moneylender?
Here's the sick squid I owe you.

What do octopuses play in their spare time?
Name that tuna.

What do you call a neurotic octopus?
A crazy, mixed-up squid.

What does an octopus wear when it's cold?
A coat of arms.

What do you get if you cross a bottle of water with an electric eel?
A bit of a shock really!

What do you get if you cross an eel with a shopper?
A slippery customer.

What's slimy, tastes of raspberry, is wobbly, and lives in the sea?
A red jellyfish.

What do you get if you cross a jellyfish with an elephant?
Jelly the Elephant.

Teacher: Martin, put some more water in the fish tank.

Martin: But, sir, they haven't drunk the water I gave them yesterday.

What is wobbly, slimy and white with red spots?

A jellyfish with measles.

One goldfish to his tankmate: If there's no god, who changes the water?

Why did the jellyfish's wife leave him?

He stung her into action.

What do you get if you cross an electric
eel and a sponge?
Shock absorbers.

What did the jellyfish say when she saw
the electric eel?
How shocking!

How do eels get around the seabed?
They go by octobus.

What's wet and wiggly and says "How do you do" sixteen times?
Two octopuses shaking hands.

What is an eel's favorite song?
Slip Sliding Away.

Have you heard the joke about the slippery eel?
You wouldn't grasp it.

What is a sea monster's favorite dish?
Fish and ships.

What did the Loch Ness Monster say to his friend?
Long time, no sea.

What is an octopus?
An eight-sided cat.

There once was a lonely young jellyfish.
Who then met a sweet, loving shellyfish.
They went with the motion
Of waves in the ocean.
And became better known as the jollyfish.

Girl: Do you know what family the octopus belongs to?
Boy: No one in our street.

Did you hear about the man who tried to cross the Loch Ness Monster with a goat?
He had to get a new goat.

Did you hear about the stupid jellyfish?
It set!

Knock, knock.
Who's there?
Eel.
Eel who?
Eel meet again.

Doctor, doctor, I feel like an electric eel.
That's shocking.

What happened when one jellyfish met another?
They produced jelly babies.

One day, a boy was walking down the street when he saw a sea monster standing on the corner looking lost. The boy put a lead on the sea monster and took him to the police station. "You should take him to the museum," said the police sergeant.
The next day the police sergeant saw the boy in the town still with the monster on a lead. "I thought I told you to take him to the museum," said the policeman.
"I did," said the boy, "and today I'm taking him to the movies."

What do you get if you cross the Loch
Ness Monster with a shark?
Loch Jaws.

What eats its victims two by two?
Noah's Shark.

How do you communicate with the Loch
Ness Monster at 20,000 fathoms?
Drop him a line.

What fish tastes best with cream?
A jellyfish.

What sort of fish performs surgical operations?
A sturgeon.

Mrs Turbot, the biology teacher, was very fond of fish. She was also rather deaf, which was great for the children in her class. What Mrs Turbot needs, said one of her colleagues, is a herring-aid.

The vampire went into the Monster Cafe. "Shark and chips," he ordered. "And make it snappy."

Teacher's
Pests

A pharmacist, a storekeeper and a teacher were sentenced to death by firing squad. The pharmacist was taken from his cell and, as the soldiers took aim, he shouted "Avalanche!" The soldiers panicked and in the confusion the pharmacist escaped. The storekeeper was led out next. As the soldiers took aim he shouted "Flood!" and escaped. The teacher was then led out. The squad took aim and the teacher, remembering how the other two had escaped, shouted "Fire!"

Teachers nowadays specialize so much that they know more and more about less and less until they know everything about nothing!

Why did the teacher have her hair in a bun?
Because she had her nose in a hamburger.

Teacher: I'd like a room, please.
Hotel Receptionist: Single, Sir?
Teacher: Yes, but I am engaged.

Mother: Why do you call your teacher "Treasure"?
Girl: Because we wonder where she was dug up.

Generally speaking, teachers are generally speaking.

"I'm not going to school today," Alexander said to his mother. "The teachers bully me and the boys in my class don't like me."

"You're going. And that's final. I'll give you two good reasons why."

"Why?"

"Firstly, you're 35 years old. Secondly, you're the principal."

Girl: My teacher's a peach.
Mother: You mean she's sweet.
Girl: No, she has a heart of stone.

Why did the teacher wear a life jacket at night?
Because she liked sleeping on a water bed, and couldn't swim!

Knock, knock.
Who's there?
Genoa.
Genoa who?
Genoa good teacher?

A motorist approached the principal one afternoon and said, "I'm awfully sorry, but I think I've just run over the school cat. Can I replace it?"
The principal looked him up and down and replied, "I doubt if you'd be the mouser she was."

What's the difference between a railroad guard and a teacher?
One minds the train, the other trains the mind.

How can a teacher increase the size of her pay check?
By looking at it through a magnifying glass.

What should a teacher take if he's run down?
The number of the car that hit him.

Teacher, in pet shop: I'd like to buy a canary, please. How much do they cost?
Pet shop owner: $10 apiece.
Teacher, horrified: How much does a whole one cost?

Why is a complaining teacher the easiest to satisfy?
Because nothing satisfies them.

What do you get if you cross your least favorite teacher with a telescope?
A horroscope.

Teacher's Pests

Miss Smith and Mrs Brown were having a chat over a cup of tea about why they entered the teaching profession. "I used to be a fortuneteller before I became a teacher," said Miss Smith. "But I had to give it up, there wasn't any future in it."

The young teacher was complaining to her friends about how badly she was being paid. "We get a really poultry amount each month," she said.

"You mean 'paltry'," corrected one of her friends.

"No I don't, I mean 'poultry'," replied the teacher. "What I earn is chicken feed."

Why can't the deaf teacher be sent to prison?
Because you can't condemn someone without a hearing.

A teacher went into a shoe store. "I'd like some crocodile shoes, please," she said.
"Certainly, Madam," said the salesgirl.
"How big is your crocodile?"

What's the difference between a caretaker and a bad-tempered teacher?
Is there any difference?

Did you hear about the cross-eyed teacher who had no control over her pupils?

What's the difference between a schoolteacher and a train?
A schoolteacher says, "Spit out that toffee" and a train says, "Choo, choo."

Did you hear about the teacher who married the dairymaid?
It didn't last. They were like chalk and cheese.

What did the teacher say after spending thousands in the expensive hotel?
I'm sorry to leave, now that I've almost bought the place.

Principal: If you liked your pupils you'd take them to the zoo.
Teacher: Oh, I know some of them come from sub-standard houses, but they can't be that bad, surely.

Why is a man wearing sunglasses like a rotten teacher?
Because he keeps his pupils in the dark.

"You can have that brain there for $5,000," said the brain surgeon to the man who was going to have a brain transplant. "It used to belong to a bank manager. This one's $5,000 too: it was a dancer's. And this one's $50,000: it belonged to a school teacher."

"Why's it ten times more than the others?" gasped the man.

"It's been used ten times less than theirs!"

Why did the Cyclops give up teaching? Because he only had one pupil.

Why did the teacher decide to become an electrician?
To get a bit of light relief.

I'm not saying our teacher's fat, but every time he falls over he rocks himself to sleep trying to get back up.

"Don't worry, Miss Jones," said the principal to the new teacher. "You'll cope with your new class, but they'll keep you on your toes."
"How's that, Sir?" asked the teacher.
"They always put thumbtacks on the chairs."

How did the teacher knit a suit of armor?
She used steel wool.

Did you hear about the man who took up
monster baiting for a living?
He used to be a teacher but he lost his
nerve.

Why are teachers happy at Halloween
parties?
Because there's lots of school spirit.

"Teacher is a bore!" was scrawled on the blackboard one day. "I do not want to see that on my blackboard," he thundered when he saw it.

"Sorry, Sir! I didn't realize you wanted it kept secret."

What's the difference between teachers and candy?
People like candy.

How did the teacher forecast the weather with a piece of string?
She hung it up, and if it moved, she knew it was windy, and if it got wet, she knew it was raining.

Why did the teacher fix her bed to the chandelier?
Because she was a light sleeper.

Did you hear about the teacher who retired?
His class gave him an illuminated address.
They burned his house down.

A teacher was being interviewed for a new job and asked the principal what the hours were. "We try to have early hours you know. I hope that suits."
"Of course," said the teacher. "I don't mind how early I leave."

What's the difference between a boring teacher and a boring book? You can shut the book up.

The principal was interviewing a new teacher. "You'll get $10,000 to start, with $15,000 after six months."
"Oh!" said the teacher. "I'll come back in six months then."

What is brown, hairy, wears dark glasses and carries a pile of exercise books?
A coconut disguised as a teacher.

"What do you do?" a man asked a very attractive girl at a party.
"I'm an infant teacher."
"Good gracious! I thought you were at least twenty-six."

What do you call a deaf teacher?
Anything you like, he can't hear you.

What do you call a teacher floating on a raft in the sea?
Bob.

Two elderly teachers were talking over old times and saying how much things had changed. "I mean," said the first, "I caught one of the boys kissing one of the girls yesterday."

"Extraordinary," said the second. "I didn't even kiss my wife before I married her, didn't you?"

"I can't remember. What was her maiden name?"

Why are art galleries like retirement homes for teachers?
Because they're both full of old masters.

Teacher's strong; teacher's gentle.
Teacher's kind. And I am mental.

Why did the teacher put corn in his shoes?
Because he had pigeon toes.

What takes a lot of licks from a teacher
without complaint?
An ice cream.

How can a teacher double his money?
By folding it in half.

How do teachers dress in mid-January?
Quickly.

Why did the mean teacher walk around
with her purse open?
She'd read there was going to be some
change in the weather.

Birds

What's the difference between a fly and a bird?
A bird can fly but a fly can't bird.

Why did the sparrow fly into the library?
It was looking for bookworms.

What do you call a snake that is trying to become a bird?
A feather boa.

What do two lovesick owls say when it's raining?
Too-wet-to-woo!

What sits in a tree and says, "Hoots, mon. Hoots, mon?"
A Scottish owl.

Why were the mommy and daddy owls worried about their son?
Because he didn't seem to give a hoot anymore.

What does an educated owl say?
Whom.

Why did the owl 'owl?
Because the Woodpecker would peck 'er.

What do confused owls say?
Too-whit-to-why?

What did the owl say to his friend as he flew off?
Owl be seeing you later.

What did the baby owl's parents say when
he wanted to go to a party?
You're not owld enough.

What did the owls do when one of them
had a punk haircut?
They hooted with laughter.

What do Scottish owls sing?
Owld Lang Syne.

What did the scornful owl say?
Twit twoo.

How do you know you are haunted by a parrot?
He keeps saying, "oooo's a pretty boy then?"

How do you know that owls are cleverer than chickens?
Have you ever heard of Kentucky Fried Owl?

What do you get if you cross King Kong with a budgie?
A messy cage.

What do you get if you cross an owl with a witch?
A bird that's ugly but doesn't give a hoot.

1st man: My wife eats like a bird.
2nd man: You mean she hardly eats a thing?
1st man: No, she eats slugs and worms.

Knock, knock.
Who's there?
Owl.
Owl who?
Owl I can say is "Knock, knock!"

Knock, knock.
Who's there?
Owl.
Owl who?
Owl be sad if you don't let me in.

Knock, knock.
Who's there?
Owl.
Owl who?
Owl aboard!

Knock, knock.
Who's there?
Baby Owl.
Baby Owl who?
Baby Owl see you later, baby not.

Two owls were playing pool.
One said, "Two hits."
The other replied, "Two hits to who?"

Why did the vulture cross the road?
For a fowl reason.

Why don't vultures fly south in the winter?
Because they can't afford the air fare.

Why did a man's pet vulture not make a
sound for five years?
It was stuffed.

What do you call a team of vultures playing
football?
Fowl play.

Where do the toughest vultures come from?
Hard-boiled eggs.

Where do vultures meet for coffee?
In a nest-cafe.

What do you call a vulture with no beak?
A head-banger.

Why couldn't the vulture talk to the dove?
Because he didn't speak pidgin English.

How do we know vultures are religious?
Because they're birds of prey.

What do a vulture, a pelican and a taxman
have in common?
Big bills!

What happened when a doctor crossed a parrot with a vampire?
It bit his neck, sucked his blood and said, "Who's a pretty boy, then?"

A woodpecker was pecking a hole in a tree. All of a sudden a flash of lightning struck the tree to the ground. The woodpecker looked bemused for a moment and then said: "Gee, I guess I don't know my own strength."

Why does a stork stand on one leg?
Because it would fall over if it lifted the other one.

Teacher: Who can tell me what geese eat?
Paul: Er, gooseberries, Sir?

Dave: The trouble with our teachers is
that they all do bird impressions.
Mave: Really? What do they do?
Dave: They watch us like hawks.

Doctor, doctor, my wife thinks she's a
duck.
You better bring her in to see me straight
away.
I can't do that – she's already flown south
for the winter.

A monster decided to become a TV star,
so he went to see an agent.
"What do you do?" asked the agent.
"Bird impressions," said the monster.
"What kind of bird impressions?"
"I eat worms."

Which bird is always out of breath?
A puffin.

What's the difference between a
gymnastics teacher and a duck?
One goes quick on its legs, the other goes
quack on its legs.

Did you hear about the village idiot buying bird seed?
He said he wanted to grow some birds.

Teacher, in pet shop: I'd like to buy a budgie, please. How much do they cost?
Pet shop owner: $10 apiece.
Teacher, horrified: How much does a whole one cost?

Teacher: What's a robin?
John: A bird that steals, Miss.

Donald: My canary died of flu.
Dora: I didn't know canaries got flu.
Donald: Mine flew into a car.

John: Why is the sky so high?
Jim: So the birds won't bang their heads.

More Really Good Knock, Knock Jokes

Knock knock.
Who's there?
Chuck.
Chuck who?
Chuck in a sandwich for lunch!

Knock knock.
Who's there?
Cliff.
Cliff who?
Cliffhanger.

Knock knock.
Who's there?
Cohen.
Cohen who?
Cohen your way.

More Really Good Knock, Knock Jokes

Knock knock.
Who's there?
Colin.
Colin who?
Colin all cars . . . Colin all cars . . .

Knock knock.
Who's there?
Cosmo.
Cosmo who?
Cosmo trouble than you're worth.

Knock knock.
Who's there?
Costas.
Costas who?
Costas a fortune to get here.

Knock knock.
Who's there?
Craig.
Craig who?
Craig in the wall.

Knock knock.
Who's there?
Crispin.
Crispin who?
Crispin crunchy is how I like my cereal.

Knock knock.
Who's there?
Cyril.
Cyril who?
Cyril animals at the zoo.

Knock knock.
Who's there?
Dale.
Dale who?
Dale come if you call dem.

Knock knock.
Who's there?
Danny.
Danny who?
Dannybody home?

Knock knock.
Who's there?
Darren.
Darren who?
Darren the garden, hiding.

Knock knock.
Who's there?
Dave.
Dave who?
Dave of glory.

Knock knock.
Who's there?
Derek.
Derek who?
Derek get richer and the poor get poorer.

Knock knock.
Who's there?
Desi.
Desi who?
Desi take sugar?

Knock knock.
Who's there?
Devlin.
Devlin who?
Devlin a red dress.

Knock knock.
Who's there?
Dewey.
Dewey who?
Dewey stay or do we go now?

Knock knock.
Who's there?
Diego.
Diego who?
Diego before de "B".

Knock knock.
Who's there?
Flo.
Flo who?
Flo your candles out.

Knock knock.
Who's there?
Flora.
Flora who?
Florat the top of the block.

Knock knock.
Who's there?
Flossie.
Flossie who?
Flossie your teeth every day.

Knock knock.
Who's there?
Francoise.
Francoise who?
Francoise once a great empire.

Knock knock.
Who's there?
Gail.
Gail who?
Gail of laughter.

Knock knock.
Who's there?
Germaine.
Germaine who?
Germaine you don't recognize me?

Knock knock.
Who's there?
Gertie.
Gertie who?
Gertiesy call!

Knock knock.
Who's there?
Gilda.
Gilda who?
Gilda the picture frame.

Knock knock.
Who's there?
Giselle.
Giselle who?
Gisellegant and very pretty.

Knock knock.
Who's there?
Gita.
Gita who?
Gita job!

Knock knock.
Who's there?
Gladys.
Gladys who?
Gladys letter isn't a bill.

Knock knock.
Who's there?
Grace.
Grace who?
Grace skies are over us.

Knock knock.
Who's there?
Greta.
Greta who?
Greta life.

Knock knock.
Who's there?
Guinevere.
Guinevere who?
Guinevere going to get together?

Knock knock.
Who's there?
Hannah.
Hannah who?
Hannah cloth out to dry.

Knock knock.
Who's there?
Harriet.
Harriet who?
Harriet up!

Knock knock.
Who's there?
Hazel.
Hazel who?
Hazel restrict your vision.

Knock knock.
Who's there?
Heather.
Heather who?
Heather pothtman come yet?

Knock knock.
Who's there?
Hedda.
Hedda who?
Hedda ball in goal.

Knock knock.
Who's there?
Carrie.
Carrie who?
Carrie on with what you are doing.

Knock knock.
Who's there?
Cassie.
Cassie who?
Cassie you some time?

Knock knock.
Who's there?
Cecile.
Cecile who?
Cecile the envelope.

Knock knock.
Who's there?
Celeste.
Celeste who?
Celeste time I come calling.

Knock knock.
Who's there?
Cindy.
Cindy who?
Cindy parcel special delivery.

Knock knock.
Who's there?
Clara.
Clara who?
Clara space on the table.

Knock knock.
Who's there?
Colleen.
Colleen who?
Colleen yourself up, you're a mess!

Knock knock.
Who's there?
Courtney.
Courtney who?
Courtney robbers lately?

Knock knock.
Who's there?
Cynthia.
Cynthia who?
Cynthia won't listen, I'll keep shouting.

Knock knock.
Who's there?
Dana.
Dana who?
Dana you mind.

Knock knock.
Who's there?
Daryl.
Daryl who?
Daryl be the day.

Knock knock.
Who's there?
Dawn.
Dawn who?
Dawn do anything I wouldn't do.

Knock knock.
Who's there?
Della.
Della who?
Della tell ya that I love ya?

Knock knock.
Who's there?
Delphine.
Delphine who?
Delphine fine, thanks.

Knock knock.
Who's there?
Denise.
Denise who?
Denise are above de feet.

Knock knock.
Who's there?
Diana.
Diana who?
Diana thirst – a glass of water, please.

Knock knock.
Who's there?
Dolly.
Dolly who?
Dolly't them in, they're dangerous.

Knock knock.
Who's there?
Donna.
Donna who?
Donna you know? Isa Luigi.

Knock knock.
Who's there?
Dora.
Dora who?
Dora steel.

Knock knock.
Who's there?
Ken.
Ken who?
Ken you come and play?

Knock knock.
Who's there?
Kenneth.
Kenneth who?
Kenneth three little kittens come out to play?

Knock knock.
Who's there?
Kevin.
Kevin who?
Kevin and sit down.

Knock knock.
Who's there?
Kurt.
Kurt who?
Kurt and wounded.

Knock knock.
Who's there?
Kyle.
Kyle who?
Kyle be good if you let me in!

Knock knock.
Who's there?
Larry.
Larry who?
Larry up.

Knock knock.
Who's there?
Laurie.
Laurie who?
Laurie-load of goods.

Knock knock.
Who's there?
Len.
Len who?
Len us a fiver will you?

Knock knock.
Who's there?
Leon.
Leon who?
Leon me – I'll support you.

Knock knock.
Who's there?
Les.
Les who?
Les see what we can do.

Knock knock.
Who's there?
Lester.
Lester who?
Lester we forget.

Knock knock.
Who's there?
Lewis.
Lewis who?
Lewis all my money in a poker game.

Knock knock.
Who's there?
Lionel.
Lionel who?
Lionel roar if you stand on its tail.

Knock knock.
Who's there?
Lloyd.
Lloyd who?
Lloyd him away with an ice-cream.

Knock knock.
Who's there?
Lou.
Lou who?
Lou's your money on the horses.

Knock knock.
Who's there?
Luke.
Luke who?
Luke through the peep-hole and you'll see.

Knock knock.
Who's there?
Luther.
Luther who?
Luther please – not tho tight!

Knock knock.
Who's there?
Lyle.
Lyle who?
Lyle low until the cops have gone.

Knock knock.
Who's there?
Malcolm.
Malcolm who?
Malcolm outside and play!

Knock knock.
Who's there?
Margo.
Margo who?
Margo, you're not needed now.

Knock knock.
Who's there?
Maria.
Maria who?
Marial name is Mary.

Knock knock.
Who's there?
Marian.
Marian who?
Mariand her little lamb.

Knock knock.
Who's there?
Marie.
Marie who?
Marie for love.

Knock knock.
Who's there?
Marietta.
Marietta who?
Marietta whole loaf!

Knock knock.
Who's there?
Marilyn.
Marilyn who?
Marilyn, she'll make you a good wife.

Knock knock.
Who's there?
Marion.
Marion who?
Marion idiot and repent at leisure.

Knock knock.
Who's there?
Martha.
Martha who?
Martha boys next door are hurting me!

Knock knock.
Who's there?
Mary.
Mary who?
That's what I keep wondering.

Knock knock.
Who's there?
Maude.
Maude who?
Mauden my job's worth.

Knock knock.
Who's there?
Mavis.
Mavis who?
Mavis be the best day of your life.

Knock knock.
Who's there?
Maxine.
Maxine who?
Maxine a lot of things.

Knock knock.
Who's there?
May.
May who?
Maybe it's a friend at the door.

Knock knock.
Who's there?
Maya.
Maya who?
Maya turn.

Knock knock.
Who's there?
Meg.
Meg who?
Meg a fuss.

Knock knock.
Who's there?
Megan.
Megan who?
Megan a loud noise.

Knock knock.
Who's there?
Michelle.
Michelle who?
Michelle has sounds of the sea
in it.

Knock knock.
Who's there?
Mimi.
Mimi who?
Mimi b-bicycle's b-broken.

Knock knock.
Who's there?
Minnie.
Minnie who?
Minnie people want to come in.

Knock knock.
Who's there?
Miranda.
Miranda who?
Miranda friend want to come in.

Knock knock.
Who's there?
Una.
Una who?
Yes, Una who.

Knock knock.
Who's there?
Utica.
Utica who?
(*sing*) "Utica high road and I'll take the low road."

Knock knock.
Who's there?
Vanda.
Vanda who?
Vanda you vant me to come round?

Knock knock.
Who's there?
Vanessa.
Vanessa who?
Vanessa time I'll ring the bell.

Knock knock.
Who's there?
Viola.
Viola who?
Viola sudden you don't know who I am?

Knock knock.
Who's there?
Violet.
Violet who?
Violet the cat out of the bag.

Knock knock.
Who's there?
Wendy.
Wendy who?
Wendy come to take you away
I won't stop them!

Knock knock.
Who's there?
Willa.
Willa who?
Willa present make you happy?

Knock knock.
Who's there?
Winnie.
Winnie who?
Winnie is better than losing.

Knock knock.
Who's there?
Xena.
Xena who?
Xena minute!

Knock knock.
Who's there?
Yvette.
Yvette who?
Yvette helps lots of animals.

Knock knock.
Who's there?
Yvonne.
Yvonne who?
Yvonne to know vat you are doing.

Knock knock.
Who's there?
Zoe.
Zoe who?
Zoe said that, did he? Don't believe him.

Knock knock.
Who's there?
Aaron.
Aaron who?
Aaron the chest means strength in arms.

Knock knock.
Who's there?
Abel.
Abel who?
Abel to go to work.

Knock knock.
Who's there?
Adair.
Adair who?
Adair you to open this door.

Knock knock.
Who's there?
Adam.
Adam who?
Adam nuisance come to borrow some sugar.